THE SPACE
ACTIVITY BOOK

By Ellen Booth Church   **Illustrated by Phil Scheuer**

Scholastic Inc.
New York   Toronto   London   Auckland   Sydney

Ellen Booth Church taught kindergarten and pre-kindergarten for 12 years. She is currently an educational consultant for K and pre-K programs nationwide, specializing in developmentally appropriate kindergarten curriculum and full-day kindergarten programming. Ms. Church has written for and served as a consultant for *Let's Find Out* since 1972. She lives joyously in the mountains of upstate New York, where the sky is so dark at night that you think you can reach up and touch the stars.

OTHER BOOKS BY ELLEN BOOTH CHURCH

Learning Things, Fearon Teacher Aids
What Works? Problem Solving, Monday Morning Books
What's This? Creative Thinking, Monday Morning Books
What Fits? Classification, Monday Morning Books

ISBN 0-590-43325-3

Copyright © 1989 by Ellen Booth Church and Phil Scheuer. All rights reserved. Published by Scholastic Inc.

Designed by Ann Bennett

4/9

12 11 10 9 8 7 6 5 4 3   Printed in the U.S.A.   08

First Scholastic printing, August 1989

WHY SPACE?

Themes in kindergarten generate excitement and help children to focus their thinking. Space is a good theme because, like dinosaurs, it is something that most children are fascinated with. Also, the scientific nature of the theme gives kindergarten teachers an opportunity to focus on science experiments. Yet it is important to remember the theme of "Space" is mainly a vehicle for process learning. The processes children use with the content information is more important than learning the "facts." The goal of a unit on Space is not for children to memorize the names of the planets or know the speed of light. Instead, the goal is for the children to use a variety of process and thinking skills in relation to a topic that peaks their interest. What children <u>do</u> with the space information is more important than what they know. The activities in this book encourage children to use creative thinking and problem solving skills in all the subject areas.

THE SCIENTIFIC METHOD

The Space Unit is a perfect opportunity for children to experience the scientific method. Interestingly, children take to the scientific method quickly because of their natural curiosity. Many of the activities in this book invite children to make predictions or hypotheses, to do experiments, and then to observe and record the results. In so doing, children see that all learning is not memorization and that they are capable of finding their own answers to problems.

ABOUT THE BOOK

The book is divided into four sections: The Sun, The Moon, The Stars and Planets, and Space Travel. It starts with a topic children are most familiar with and moves to the most unfamiliar. The Sun section gives children some grounding with activities that are the most concrete. Each successive section adds more and more abstract information for childen to experience. Yet even the most abstract activities are presented in a hands-on manner. Following this sequence will allow children to build on information and experiences as they move from one section to the next. During the unit, set aside a special investigation table for projects, books, and pictures related to the topic.

Resources For Space Education Materials

National Aeronautic and Space Administration, Education Affairs, Washington, D.C. 20546—good source for educational materials

Young Astronaut Council, 1015 15th St. N.W., Suite 905, Washington, D. C., 20005—good for information and illustrations

Student Shuttle Involvement Program, National Science Teachers Assoc., 1742 Connecticut Ave. , Washington, D.C. 20009—interesting information for children

Missionspace Teacher's Kit, Media Mart, 72 East 45th St., NY, NY 10036—materials that clearly illustrate space travel

Moon and Stars/ Sun: Science Themes II packet (David C. Cook Pub., 850 N. Grove Ave. Elgin, IL 60120)—good simple pictures

THE SUN

Children are aware of the sun, or the lack of it every day. They know it can effect their ability to play outside, but they usually don't think about the sun's importance to the earth and space. This section is designed to give children concrete experiences with the sun's effects and its role in space. The following are facts for teachers to keep in mind during this section of the Space Unit.

facts

1. The sun is a medium-sized star around which the earth and the other planets move (orbit).
2. The sun is the center of our solar system.
3. The sun holds all the planets in their position in space.
4. The sun is bigger than all the planets put together.
5. Without the sun, the solar system would be very cold and dark.

Sun Predictions

Concept: Sunlight can shine through some things.

● Talk about the sun's ability to shine through some objects. Ask children to look around the room to find any examples of the sun shining through something. Good things to look for are curtains, windowshades, fish tanks, etc. Brainstorm a chart of sunlight predictions. Have children name all the things they think sunlight can shine through. Write these on the chart, and if possible, add a small picture to illustrate each item. Now collect as many of the items as possible and test them at a sunny window or take them outside. Use a green crayon to check off all the objects that the sun shines through. Use a red crayon to cross out the objects that the sun did not shine through. Ask, "Why could the sun shine through some objects and not through others? What is the same or different about these objects?"

Sun Powered Cooking

Concept: The warmth of the sun can dry foods.

● Use firm, ripe Thompson (green) seedless grapes to make sun dried raisins. First have children weigh five grapes on a pan balance scale. Record the weight. Now have children wash and dry grapes and place on paper plates. Cover the plates with cheesecloth or screening. Place the plates on blocks so the air can circulate around the plate, and put in a sunny spot. Watch and wait for about four days. The raisins should be leathery and pliable when they are done. Weigh five raisins on the pan balance and compare to the grapes' weight. Ask, "How did the grapes change? What caused them to change? Could we make raisins in a dark place?" At snack serve both raisins and grapes for further comparisons.

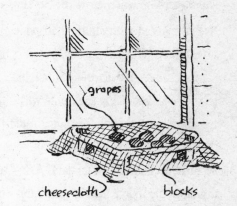

Make "Sun Tea"

● Demonstrate the warming power of the sun by making some herbal tea for snack. Fill a clear glass quart jar with water and add two herbal tea bags. Cover tightly and place in the sun for two to three hours. Periodically check the jar for changes in the color of the water. Make a color chart of these observed changes. Have children use crayons to color in outline drawings of the jar. Sequence these pictures from left to right to form a solar tea chart. Serve the tea over ice with honey and lemon for snack.

Measuring Melting

Concept: The warmth of the sun can melt some things faster than others.

● Experiment with melting. Provide children with a variety of objects to melt in the sun. Use items such as ice cubes, butter, peanut butter, chocolate, small crayons, and birthday candles. Make predictions about which ones will melt slow and which will melt fast. Make a picture chart showing the items with a fast and slow box next to each. Have children check the appropriate boxes for their predictions. Next, place the items on paper plates and put them on a sunny windowsill or outside in the direct sun. Observe the melting speed and record the results on the chart. Ask, "Which items melted the fastest? Which items melted the slowest? Why? Would they melt on a cloudy day?" Try it!

Measuring Evaporation

Concept: We can measure the way the sun drys (evaporates) things.

● Pour a quarter cup of water on the center of a large sheet of dark construction paper. Watch the paper absorb the water. Take chalk or a white crayon and draw along the outside edge of spot. This represents the starting size of the spot. Now place the paper in the sun to dry. Every few minutes check the paper to see if the size of the spot has changed. Use the chalk to outline the new size of the water spot. Continue this until the water spot has totally evaporated. The paper will have a series of concentric circles that represent the evaporation process.

Evaporate A Glass Of Water

● Fill two large plastic glasses with equal amounts of water. Place one in the sun and the other in a dark place. Predict which glass of water will evaporate first. Make a yarn graph to represent the evaporation "race." Cut a piece of yellow or red yarn the same height as the water in the "sun" glass. Then cut a piece of black or blue yarn the same height as the water in the other glass. Place the yarn side by side on a graph. Every day measure the two glasses with the different color yarn and place the yarn pieces on the graph. Notice which glass is evaporating faster. Why?

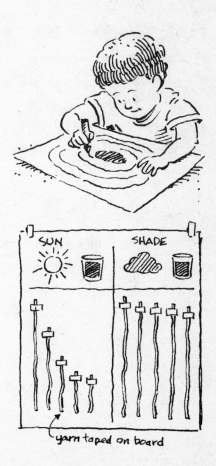

yarn taped on board

Create A Class Book

Concept: We need the sun to help us live on the earth.

● Present an open ended question to encourage problem solving. Remember when asking an open ended question to accept all answers equally. The purpose of this activity is not to get the "right" answer but to provide an opportunity for creative thinking and language skills. Ask, "What would happen if the sun didn't shine? How would the world be different?" Discuss what the world would probably look like, what people, animals, and plants would be here, etc. Have children think about what all living things would have to do to adapt to the new environment. (This is an excellent way to assess how much children know about the function of the sun.) To help make the discussion more concrete, talk about the difference between the way a sunny or cloudy day feels. Help children notice the change in temperature, light, etc. Give children paper to draw their idea of what the world would look like if the sun didn't shine. Then have them write or dictate their ideas. Bind these together into a class book entitled: *The Day the Sun Stopped Shining*.

Sun Poetry

● Encourage children to use descriptive language as they brainstorm different words to describe the sun. Invite children to first think of words that describe how the sun looks, then how it feels. Encourage children to think of many different words that describe the sun. Ask, "Can you think of another word to say the same thing?" Use these words to form a "shape" poem. Lightly outline the shape of the sun on chart paper. Write their words on the outline so that the finished poem will be a collection of words in the shape of the shining sun.

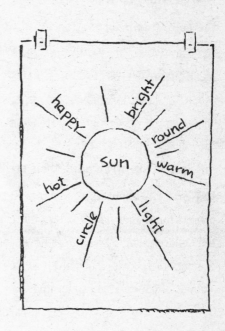

Recommended Read-Aloud Books

Sun, Michael Ricketts (Grosset and Dunlap) — sunlight and what it does for us

The Day the Sun Danced, Edith Hurd (Harper & Row) — the sun and its effect on the coming of spring

Sunshine Makes the Seasons, Franklyn M. Branley (Crowell) — simple, readable explanation of how sunshine and the earth's orbit effects the seasons

Play With the Sun, Howard E. Smith (McGraw-Hill) — informational activities that clearly explain sun and light

Vermont Farm and the Sun, Constance and Raymond Montgomery (Vermont Crossroads Press) — excellent photos and simple words explain the sun as a source of energy

Our Friend the Sun, Janet Palazzo (Troll Assoc.) — Simple book about the sun's benefits

Sun Occupations

Concept: Some occupations study the sun, others need the sun to do their work.

● Ask, "Who works with the sun? What jobs study the sun? What jobs need the sun to make them successful?" First, focus on weather forecasters. Explain that their job is to watch the weather and predict if it will be sunny or cloudy in the next few days. For "homework," have children watch television weather forecasters to see what they do. Have the children pretend to be weather forecasters and predict the number of sunny days for the next week. Write down their predictions and check them at the end of the week.

● Next, talk about astronomers. Explain that their job is to watch the sun, stars, and planets for changes and to learn more about things that happen in space. It is important to tell children that astronomers never look directly at the sun. It is so hot and bright that it can hurt their eyes. They always focus a telescope so that it makes a picture of the sun on a sheet of paper. If possible, invite an astronomer to visit. Talk about other jobs that are more indirectly related to the sun. Farmers, for example, need the sun to grow their crops, a life guard needs sunny days to work at a pool or ocean, an outdoor carnival or circus needs the sun to attract crowds, etc. What other jobs need the sun to be successful?

Solar Pictures

Concept: The sun's light can change colors.

● Bring in pieces of clothing, papers, books, etc. that have been faded by the sun. Look for faded items in the classroom. Talk about what happened to the objects. Ask, "How did these objects change?" Explain that the light of the sun has the ability to change colors. Have children look at home for more examples of the sun's fading power.

● Tell children that with this art project they can make a picture without paint, crayons, markers, or glue. The sun is going to do all the work! On a bright day have children place dark construction paper (black, blue, or purple) on a sunny windowsill. Then have them collect interesting objects to arrange in a pattern on the paper. Good things to use are paper clips, cookie cutters, manipulative pieces, and keys. Some children may also want to cut out cardboard geometric shapes or silhouettes. Have children place them in an arrangement or pattern on top of the construction paper and leave it in the sun for several days. Encourage children to carefully check on their picture's progress every few days. Eventually they will have a faded background picture with dark objects silhouetted on it.

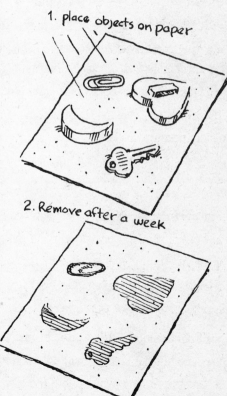

1. place objects on paper

2. Remove after a week

Solar Blueprint Pictures

● This is a great outdoor activity for a sunny day. Use blueprint paper (inexpensive and found at blueprint or architect companies) to make another type of solar picture. Fill a large covered container like a saucepan or gallon jar with about ⅓ to ½ cup of ammonia. Have children collect natural objects such as flowers, grasses, and seed pods to place on the paper. In a shady place have children arrange their objects in a design on a sheet of blueprint paper that has been placed on a flat board. Next expose the paper to the sun for about fifteen to twenty seconds. Now remove the objects and roll the paper up. Place the paper inside the ammonia container for about a minute, remove, and unroll. The seemingly solid-colored piece of paper will now show the outline of the nature objects!

Sun Clay

Sun Clay

Ingredients:

2/3 cup water	1/2 cup water
2 cups salt	1 cup cornstarch

● Place salt in pot, add ⅔ cup water, stir and cook over medium heat for about 5 minutes. The salt will dissolve. Cool. In separate container, slowly mix ½ cup water and cornstarch. When smooth, mix with the salt mixture, place on low heat and cook until it starts to get thick and smooth. Allow to cool. This clay is excellent for modeling because it can be hardened in the sun but will not crumble like playdough. Invite children to create suns, moons, stars, and planets with the clay. Provide pictures of planets and the solar system for inspiration. Toothpicks, seeds, beans, pipe cleaners, etc. are excellent for decoration.

Dance Around The Sun

Concept: The sun is not solid like the earth. It is a huge ball of fiery gases.

● Talk about the appearance of the sun. From the earth it looks like a big ball. Explain that the sun is not solid but really a collection of spinning hot gases. These gases appear to be white, yellow, red, and orange. Sometimes giant spurts of gas explode off the surface of the sun. These are called solar flares. This effect makes the suface of the sun appear to be bubbling like boiling water. Give children red, yellow, white, and orange steamers or scarves to imitate the action of the gases on the surface of the moon. Have children sit in concentric circles of colors. The center circle is the white streamers (the hottest part of the sun). The next circle is yellow, then orange, and the last circle is red. Ask the children to stand up. Put on some movement music and invite children to "boil and bubble" around in their circles to the music. The circles can spin in different directions. Periodically say "solar flare," at which time the red streamers burst off the circle and then return to their place. To end the activity, have children slowly "run out of gas" and sit on the floor as you gradually turn down the volume of the music.

Recommended Background Music

Silk Road, **or** *The Light of the Spirit,* **or any other recording by Kitaro (Geffen Records)**
Caverna Magica, **Andreas Vollenweider (CBS Records)**

The Sun Shadow Game

Concept: Shadows are formed when sunlight is blocked.

● Play a shadow movement game. Divide the group into "suns" and "shadows." Give half the class cut-out "sun tags" (yellow circles) to wear, the other half "shadow tags" (black circles). Partner suns with shadows. Shadow children imitate whatever the sun does. Later children switch tags and roles. Add soft background music and encourage children to move around the room with their shadow.

THE MOON

the moon is a friendly, familiar sight to children. They enjoy watching it change and like to tell stories about the "Man in the Moon." Yet young children have very little information about this wonderful ball they see in the sky at night. The activities in this section provide children with an opportunity to experiment with some facts about the moon. The following facts are background for teachers.

facts

1. The moon is the closest object to the earth, yet it is still very far away.

2. If a car could drive to the moon, it would take it 5 months of driving without stopping to get there.

3. Nothing will grow on the moon because there is no air or water there.

4. The moon doesn't make its own light. It shines because it reflects the light of the sun.

5. The moon is completely silent because there is no air to carry sound. Someone could pop a balloon behind you and you would not hear it.

GREEN CHEESE

The Phases Of The Moon

Concept: **The moon appears to change shape, but it doesn't really. It only looks that way. From the earth we only see the part of the moon that is lit up by the sun.**

● Talk about the moon. Ask children to tell about anything they have noticed about the moon. If available, read *Wait Till the Moon is Full,* by Margaret Wise Brown (Harper & Row). The delightful storyline clearly describes the process of waiting for a full moon. Show pictures (cut-out black silhouettes) of the different phases and discuss their names: New-Moon, Crescent, Half Moon, Full-Moon. Make a calendar chart representing the phases of the moon. Starting on the next full moon, ask children to observe the moon in the evening before they go to bed. In school have children choose the correct picture to represent what they saw and place it on the calendar. The whole process will take about a month from full moon to full moon. Ask, "Can you see the moon during the day?" Take a walk outside at different times of the day to see.

Comparing The Moon And The Earth

Concept: The moon is smaller than the earth. It would take 50 moons to fill up a ball the same size as the earth.

● It takes fifty moons to equal the size of the earth. Ask, "How many is 50?" Use counters, beans, or buttons to count out fifty in groups of ten. Then use oranges, apples, or balls to represent the 50 moons. Take a clear plastic bag and have children count out the 50 "moons" into the bag. Shape the bag into a ball and tie shut. Use colored markers to decorate the outside to look like the land and oceans of the earth. Take the "earth" around the room and look for other objects that are the same size.

Concept: The moon is smaller than the earth. It takes 81 moons to weigh one earth.

● Use a pan balance scale to help children get a perspective on the weight difference between the earth and the moon. Collect 81 sphere shaped objects (grapes, fresh peas, marbles, styrofoam balls) to represent the moon, and a few different size balls, melons, or oranges to represent the earth. Explain that our earth weighs as much as 81 moons put together. Have children count out the 81 "moon" objects on one side of the scale. Then test out which of the "earth" objects most closely balances the "moons." (It may not be totally accurate.) Invite children to find other objects that weigh the same as the "moons" or the "earth."

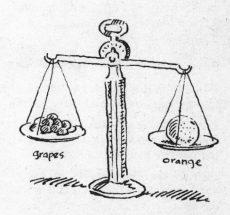

grapes   orange

What Does The Moon Look Like?

● People often say they see things when they look at the moon. Years ago, before astronauts went there, people thought the moon was made of green cheese (because of the holes). Today, some people still think they see a man in the moon, others think it looks like a giant wheat cracker. Invite children to do some pretending. After they have observed the moon during the different phases ask, "What do you see in the moon? What does it remind you of?" Have children write or dictate their ideas on a sheet of paper. Make a class moon mural. On a bulletin board, outline a large circle on black paper. Give children sponges dipped in white and grey paint to fill the circle with moon-like sponge prints. Display the children's writing around the moon and title the board: *What Does the Moon Look Like To You?*

Recommended Read-Aloud Books

Regards to the Man in the Moon, Ezra Jack Keats (Four Winds Press)—A child takes a wonderful imaginary journey to the moon.

Moon Bear, Frank Asch (Scribner's)—A little bear is afraid that the moon will disappear and never come back. Also by Frank Asch: *Happy Birthday, Moon; Mooncake;* and *Moongame.*

Wait Till the Moon is Full, Margaret Wise Brown (Harper & Row)—A little racoon has to watch and wait for the moon to be full before he joins the others in a special frolick.

Traveling To The Moon

Concept: **Astronauts landed on the moon. While they were there, they had to wear special space suits and use air tanks. They did many experiments and collected moon rocks and soil to study.**

● Talk about astronauts and their work. Have children brainstorm a list of all the things they know about astronauts. Write these on an experience chart and draw simple pictures to illustrate wherever possible. Use pictures from library books to show any other facts that they may want to know. Focus on the tools astronauts need to travel to the moon. Ask, "Why do you think they need to wear air tanks, space suits, and weighted boots?" (Because there is no air, water, and very little gravity.) Expain that the astronauts conducted experiments on the moon. They found that soil from the moon would grow plants on earth even though it couldn't on the moon. Astronauts need to train before they go into space. Talk about the special schools they must attend. For more information write to the *Young Astronaut Council, 1015 15th St. N.W., Suite 905, Washington, D.C. 20005.* Encourage children to act out astronaut roles. Provide art and junk materials for building a lunar module in the block area. Use photos of the lunar module for reference.

Moonscape Craters

Concept: The moon's surface is made of grayish, dusty rock and is covered with hills and craters (holes). Some craters are tiny and others are as big as a city. Craters were probably made by rocks that smashed into the moon long ago.

● If available, show pictures of the moon's surface and discuss its appearance. Ask, "How is the moon different from earth? How is it the same?" Use plaster of paris to create a moonscape. Mix plaster according to container directions and spread into a large pie or pizza pan. Have children shape some low hills. While the plaster is wet, tell children to gently throw different size balls or marbles into the moonscape. Then remove them and observe the crater left behind. Let it harden and then sprinkle with flour, dusting powder, or powdered gray tempera paint. In a dark place shine a flashlight on the moonscape to see how it would appear in space.

wet plaster of paris

Playing With "Moon Rocks"

Concept: Everything weighs less on the moon. Astronauts can carry huge rocks because they are as light as balloons.

● Play a weightless "Moon Rocks" game. Explain that on the moon things are much lighter than on earth. Tell children that in this game they are going to pretend to be dancing on the moon. Remind them that on the moon everybody moves in slow motion. Put on some floating or "spacey" music and invite children to move to it. Then bring out a bag of "Moon Rocks," (balloons). Now have children move to the music but at the same time try to keep their balloon up in the air. When the music stops, they have to catch their balloon and sit on the floor.

A Moon Parachute Game

● Use a parachute or large white sheet to represent the moon. Have children sit around the outside edge. Tell them that they are going to take a pretend trip to the moon and take a weightless walk there. Next have them squat in place and hold the edges of the parachute tightly with both hands. Then say a count down, "10, 9, 8, 7, 6, 5, 4, 3, 2, 1, Blast off!" At that time have children raise the parachute up in the air, high above their heads. When the parachute is up high and filled with air call two children's names to "moonwalk" underneath. When it starts to fall they must run back to the edge. Continue doing this until every child has had a chance to do a weightless walk on the "moon." Then do the count down again and return to the sitting position and "home."

STARS & PLANETS

how many times have children wished upon a star and wondered what it is? The hands-on activities in this section help children combine the fantasy and reality of stars and planets. The following facts are background for teachers.

facts

1. Stars are made of gases and give off heat and light.
2. Stars are not all the same. They are different sizes and colors.
3. Stars can be blue, white, yellow, orange, or red. (Depending on the amount of heat.)
4. Planets are farther away than the moon.
5. Planets do not give off heat or light, they only reflect the light of the sun.
6. Some planets are made of rocks and others are made of liquids.

24

Gravity Experiments

Concept: Gravity is a force that pulls us towards the earth and keeps us from falling off. There is very little gravity on the moon. There is no gravity in space.

● Gravity is a difficult concept. Avoid trying to explain it and instead give children many concrete experiments with gravity. Hold up a book and ask, "What will happen if I let go of this book? Will it go up or down?" Drop the book to demonstrate. Explain that it is the pull of gravity that makes the book fall. If the book was dropped in space it would float away. Give other examples of gravity. Go outside and have children jump from a stair, go down a slide, ride a seesaw, and hang upside down on the climbing bars to feel the pull of gravity on their body. Tell children to hold their hands above their heads. Ask, "How long can you do this? Why do your arms get tired?" Invite children to show how high they can jump. Ask, "Why can't you jump off the earth into space?"

Grow "Space Rocks"

Concept: Some planets (Venus, Mercury, Earth, Mars, and Pluto) are made of rocks and gases.

● Tell children that some planets are made of rock and others are a combination of liquids and gases. The earth is a planet that is made of rocks and gases. Some of the rocks and gases on other planets are different from the earth's rocks. Explain that we can create or "grow" our own space rocks in school. Even though they are not exactly like the ones on the planets, they are similar. Give each child a paper cup and a plastic spoon. Tell them to fill the cup half way with water. Then have them slowly stir in salt. Have them continue this until the salt no longer dissolves and starts to sink to the bottom of the cup. Next have them add a teaspoon of vinegar and a small piece of coal or pumous stone to the cup. Watch the cups over the next few days for the growth of crystal "space rocks" on the coal.

Discovering Distance

Concept: Everything we see in the sky is very, very far away. Some stars are as big as the sun but don't look that way because they are so far away. Planets look like stars because they are farther away than the moon.

● It is difficult for children to comprehend the vast distances in space. Yet they can see that distance can make things look smaller. Do this activity out on the playground or in a long hall. Ask two children of the same height to stand next to each other. Have children notice their height. Now have one child take twenty steps away from his/her partner. Ask, "Do they both look the same size now? If not, which one looks smaller?" Now have the child walk farther away. Have children watch to see if the child is getting bigger or smaller? Choose children to be the sun, moon, stars and planets. (They can hold representational pictures.) Place the moon and sun closest to the observers and then the stars and planets farther away. Show that the sun and moon look bigger than the stars and planets because they are closer.

Constellation Stories

Concept: Groups of stars are called constellations.

● Explain that constellations are groups of stars that look like dot to dot pictures in the sky (without the lines). Use good star books to show pictures of the constellations. Two good books are by H. A. Rey: *Finding the Constellations* (Houghton Mifflin), and *Know the Stars* (Scholastic). Talk about the names of the constellations. Tell children that long ago people used to tell stories about the stars. They named the constellations according to what they thought they looked like. If possible, tell one of the star stories. Invite children to create their own constellation and story. Have children draw their constellation on white paper with white crayons. (Press hard with the crayons.) Then paint thinned blue or black tempera paint over the picture. The stars will appear to "come out" in the night sky. Children can use a marker to connect their stars into a constellation.

Create Your Own Planet

Concept: Astronomers are often making new discoveries in space.

● Explain that scientists and astronomers don't know everything there is to know about space. They are constantly observing, studying, and experimenting. They often make new discoveries. Spacecrafts travel to distant planets to send back pictures and information. Ask, "What would happen if they found a new planet? What if you could create you own planet? What would it be like?" Invite children to brainstorm the things they would like to have on their planet. Tell them this is their chance to make the "perfect" planet to live on. Make a class experience chart of their ideas. Ask, "What would your planet look like? What would life be like there? What type of beings would live there? How would they eat, play, work, etc? How would people get along with each other? How would they take care of their garbage?" Next have a group of children create the new planet in the block area. First have children focus on the physical formation of the planet using the blocks, and any art or prop materials they need. Some children may want to make costumes. Then have them work out the living conditions and social interactions. Afterward, have the children show their planet to the group and tell about life there. Encourage other groups of children to make their own planet another day.

Making Binoculars And Telescopes

Concept: People use binoculars and telescopes to look at the stars and planets.

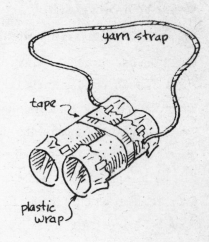

● If possible, bring in a real pair of binoculars for the children to experience. Show them how things that are far away look closer through binoculars. Explain that people often use them to observe the stars and planets. Make play binoculars. Cut small squares of clear plastic wrap and attach to the end of two toilet paper rolls with a rubber band. Next have children tape the rolls together. Then take another piece of tape and wrap it around the outside of both rolls. Provide collage materials and glue for decoration. Punch a hole on each side at the top, and string with yarn to make a neckband. Make a telescope out of a gift wrap tube or by taping two paper towel rolls together.

Space Mobile

Concept: Our part of space is called the Solar System and is filled with stars, planets, moons and the sun.

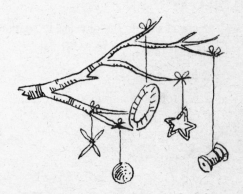

● Talk about the solar system. Ask, "What planet or star names do you know? What other things are in space?" Make a list of their answers. Show children how to make space mobiles. Provide a wide variety of junk materials for the creation of planets, stars, etc. Try using small paper plates and bowls, thread and ribbon spools, styrofoam balls, buttons, pipe cleaners, aluminum foil, toothpicks, etc. Have good pictures of the stars and planets available for reference. Hang these space objects from interesting branches, coat hangers, or dowels. Try making this activity into a giant class mobile.

Sing A Song Of Planets

Concept: The planets in our solar system orbit in an order from the Sun.

Sing a Song of Planets (Tune: Sing a Song of Sixpence)

Sing a song of planets,
going 'round the Sun.
First comes Mercury,
closest to the Sun.

Next comes Venus,
followed by Earth and Mars.
Then there's Jupiter, Saturn,
Uranus, Neptune, and Pluto.

Cooperative Musical Stars And Planets

● This game is played like a reverse musical chairs. Instead of children being left "out," children have to work together to help each other stay "in!" Ahead of time, cut large sheets of construction paper or oaktag into planet and star shapes. Make one per child. Spread the stars and planets out on the floor in a large open space. Now explain the rules of the game. Say, "This is a galaxy where all the beings work together to help each other. If anyone loses their home the others take them in. When the music starts you can walk, skip, or dance around the shapes without touching them. Then when the music stops you have to find a planet or star to stand or sit on." After the first musical "stop," take away one or more planets/stars. Remind children that the next time the music stops they need to help their friends in the galaxy that need a home planet. The game continues until there are only a few planets/stars left, and many children are huddled together on them. A great lesson in cooperation!

SPACE TRAVEL

young children are fascinated by space travel. They are very interested in space vehicles and astronauts, and enjoy making up pretend trips into space. This section provides children with an opportunity to concretely experiment with some space travel facts. Teachers can use the following facts for additional information.

facts

1. Space is so large that it never ends.
2. Everything in space is very far away.
3. There is no air, water, or gravity in space.
4. On the moon it is extremely hot during the day, and extremely cold at night.
5. Rockets have to blast off very fast to get away from the pull of the earth's gravity.

How Do Rockets Work?

Concept: Rockets are used to power space crafts into space.

● Talk about rockets and how they are used. If possible, use pictures to show the different types of rockets that have been used to get spacecrafts into space. Have children notice the smoke and air that comes out of the end of the rocket. Explain that it is this energy or power that goes down that pushes the spacecraft up in the air. Use a balloon to demonstrate this. Inflate a balloon and tie off the end. Have children try to throw it up in the air. (It won't go far.) Now inflate another balloon and let it go up in the air. (It will rise higher and faster.) Have children note how the air coming out of the end of the balloon pushes it up in the air. Inflate the balloon again, hold it so children can feel the power of the air leaving the balloon. Try making rockets. Use a small brown paper lunch bag for the spacecraft. Take a long balloon, about 7 to 10 inches, and inflate it. Put the bag on the tip of the balloon and let the balloon go. The air going out of the back of the balloon will push the "rocket" forward. Try using different weight materials to make the spacecraft. Ask, "Do some move more easily than others? Why?"

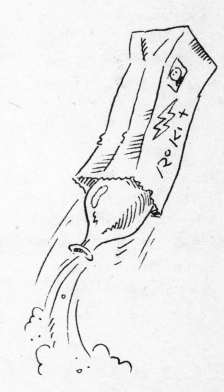

Eating In Space

Concept: Astronauts can't eat food in space the same way they do on earth because of the lack of gravity.

● Eating in space is very different than on earth. Astronauts can eat many of the same foods they normally eat on earth but they can't put the foods on plates because in the weightless atmosphere the food would float right off the plate! Many foods are placed in plastic tubes or bags. To eat, all the astronaut has to do is squeeze the food out of the bag through a straw. They also eat bite size pieces of cheese and meat that are in containers. Have the children help prepare a special "space snack." Prepare frozen orange juice. Carefully pour juice into plastic bags, insert a straw, and close with a twist tie around the bag and straw. Next make instant pudding. Have children spoon individual servings into plastic sandwich bags, insert straw, and close with a twist tie. Cut small pieces of cheese and place in plastic food containers. Serve at snack time or use the space food on a pretend class trip into space.

Take-Off Predictions

● Make comparisons about take-off distances. Have children construct different sized folded paper airplanes. Explain that these will represent different size rockets. Now invite children to make predictions of how far they think the rockets will fly when they are thrown. Place a strip of masking tape on the floor for the launch pad. Then have children place strips of tape on the floor at the place they think the rocket will land. Throw it and see whose prediction was the closest. Next try a different size paper plane. Ask children to predict whether it will land at the same place or a different one. Use tape to mark the new predictions. Continue predicting with different size "rockets." Ask, "What type of "rocket" goes the farthest? What would happen if we put a paper clip on the nose of the rocket? How far would it go?" Try it!

UFO's And Aliens

● Most children have heard of UFO's and aliens from television, books, or movies. Have a brainstorming session to discuss what their opinions are about them. Ask, "Do you think aliens and UFO's are real or pretend? Are there other beings that live in space?" Make a pro and con chart. On one side list all the reasons children think they do exist and on the other side list the reasons they think they don't. Then have children do some creative thinking and pretending. Give them large sheets of plain paper to draw what they think an alien might look like. Have them include a picture of the spacecraft, too. At the bottom of the paper save room for the children to write or dictate thoughts about their alien. Ask them to tell about what the alien looks like, what it eats, how it moves, where it lives, and even how it likes to play. Put these pages all together in a Big Book about aliens and UFO's.

Recommended Read-Aloud Books

A Book Of Astronauts for You, Franklyn Branley (Crowell)—Illustrations show their clothing and food and the inside of a space ship.

Let's Go to the Moon, Janice Knudsen Wheat (National Geographic Society)—An excellent book for showing pictures of space travel.

Magic Monsters Learn About Space, Jane Beik Moncure (Children's Press)—A fun book about space.

A Day In Space, Suzanne Lord (Scholastic)—Clearly illustrates space travel.

Is There Life In Outer Space?, Franklyn Branley (Harper & Row)—A good book for handling this question

Create A Space Ship And Mission Control

Concept: There are many different jobs related to space travel.

● Astronauts are not the only people who work in space travel. For example, there are scientists and engineers who design the rockets, ground control people who make sure the spacecraft is safe for take off, and people who work at Mission Control who talk with the astronauts in space. Have children act out these jobs in the dramatic play and block areas. Give children props to turn the dramatic play area into Mission Control. Use cardboard boxes, nuts and bolts, paper plates, aluminum foil, and junk materials to make the computers and viewing screens found there. Give children toilet paper tubes with a ball of cloth stuck in one end to use as microphones. In the meantime, have another group work on setting up the spaceship in the block area. First have children outline it with blocks and then build places to sit inside. Use art materials to make control panels and microphones. Then during activity time encourage children in the two areas to create a simulated take-off and excursion into space.

Cardboard Box Spacecraft

● Discuss the different vehicles people have used to go into space (rockets, lunar module, space shuttles). If available, show pictures from books to illustrate. Two good books are: *The Space Shuttle Action Book,* by Patrick Moore (Random House), and *Finding Out About Rockets and Spaceflight* (Usborne Explainers). Collect many large cardboard cartons. Try to find at least one that is refrigerator or washing machine size. On the first day of construction, have children design the shape of the spacecraft, cut windows and doors with help, and paint the outside with grey or silver tempera paint. The next day, provide junk materials for added detail. Use items such as aluminum foil, bottle caps, buttons, paper plates, paper towel tubes, egg cartons, styrofoam pieces, yarn for rockets, control panels, etc. Use the spacecraft for dramatic play activities.

Satellites

Concept: A satellite is an unmanned space ship that goes around the earth and sends back information.

● Talk about the things satellites do for people. Some satellites are used to study the weather. Explain how they send pictures of the weather back to earth so we can know what type of weather is coming in the next few days. Have children watch a television weather report to see satellite pictures that show cloud formations. Satellites are also used to study forest fire damage, oil spills, even farmland. A satellite acts like a giant camera in space. If available, show *A Book of Satellites for You,* by Franklyn Branley (Crowell) for good clear pictures of satellites. Make satellites with tooth picks (use double pointed ones) and dried peas. A night ahead, soak whole (not split) dried peas in a big bowl of water. Drain them the next morning. The toothpicks will easily stick into the soaked pea. Show children how to connect the peas and toothpicks together into satellite shapes. Also try using styrofoam pieces and balls.

peas

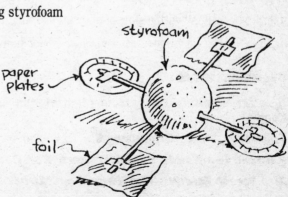

styrofoam

paper plates

foil

39

A Guided Fantasy Trip Into Space

● Take a pretend trip into space. First define the areas where the pretend spaceship and the moon will be. Sit children on the floor in the meeting time area. Invite children to tell what they think an astronaut must do to get ready to go into space. Then talk children through the trip. First tell them to get a space suit and put it on ("One leg at a time."), next the boots, ("They're heavy!"), and then the helmet, ("Have a friend help you put it on and fasten it.") Create a spaceship by putting chairs or mats in rows on the floor. Show children the door and invite them to enter. Tell them to sit down and put on their seat belts. Together say the count down and blast off. Once in space put on some "space" music and allow children to take off their seat belts and "float" around to the music. Say, "Look, just ahead is the moon. Get back to your seats for landing!" Land and have children put on their pretend air tanks and leave the ship to walk around the moon. Put on more music for them to practice walking with a slow bouncy step around the moon. When the music stops have them return to the spacecraft and blast off for home.

Recommended Music

Ride Through the Solar System, Michael Stein and Bryan Smith (Music for Little People)

Solo Flight, Marc Allen (Rising Sun Records)

Between Two Worlds, Patrick O'Hearn (RCA Records)

Also Sprach Zarathustra, (Theme from "2001"), Richard Strauss